H.P. LOVECRAFT
AND THE STARS

ALSO BY E. HOFFMANN PRICE

Operation Exile

Operation Isis

Operation Longlife

Operation Misfit

*The E. Hoffmann Price Spicy Adventure MEGAPACK™:
14 Tales from the "Spicy" Pulp Magazines!*

The Jade Enchantress

H.P. LOVECRAFT AND THE STARS

E. HOFFMANN PRICE

WILDSIDE PRESS

Originally published in *The Arkham Sampler*, Spring, 1949.
Copyright © 1949, 1977 by August Derleth. Reprinted
by permission of the E. Hoffman Price estate.
For more information, contact:
www.wildsidepress.com

LOVECRAFT AND THE STARS

Since no one thus far has been able to give me the hour and minute of Howard Phillips Lovecraft's birth in Providence, R. I., August 20, 1890, I accepted the challenge (which no full fledged astrologer would dignify by considering it as such) and set to work on the tentative assumption that he'd been born at noon. Upon erecting a chart, I noted that Venus, Uranus, and the Moon, with the two last named in conjunction, were in Libra, and in the Twelfth House.

Inasmuch as those three planets might actually have been in any one of the twelve mundane houses at the time of birth, I checked the delineations for each of the trio, and in every house. After eliminating such absurdities as "Secret love affairs, leading to enmity of women… love of horses and large animals…" (Venus in XII), and "favors from females…fruitful marriage," (Venus in XI), and "Loss of first child…inconstancy in love affairs… romantic and impulsive attachments" (Uranus in V), and "changeful relations with opposite sex…female enmity," (Moon in VII), I came to a delineation for the Third House which gave a close portrayal.

This would suggest that the time of his birth was between 4:00 a. m. and 6:00 a. m. since during those two hours, Venus, Uranus, and the Moon were in the Third House (though, of course, all in Libra; don't confuse a mundane house with a zodiacal sign, of which there are also twelve.)

Next, the Ascendant: Leo would be rising, between 4:00 a. m. and 6:00 a. m. Now, each sign is divided into three decans of ten-degrees apiece. My problem was to determine which decan was rising. The third decan was clearly not for HPL: "Capable of, and desiring command...inclined to hazardous feats...rules with a high hand, and is successful over his enemies." The HPL I knew was no such swashbuckler—neither am I, though he always tagged me as such! The second decan, ruled by Jupiter, ascribes to the native "kind, humane disposition", which HPL surely did have, and also, "artistic faculty"; but he did not have a "fortunate and profitable nature, nor fortune in speculation, nor self-confidence;" and while he "gained by legacy", he won no success through marriage. I need not have checked so closely.

Whatever his qualities were, they were not "Jovial"; he could not have been born during the rising of a decan ruled by Jupiter. But the first decan, ruled by Saturn, (and HPL was Saturnian in his writing of graves, crypts, the sinister and subterranean), was revealing.

"Strong, forceful nature, difficult to control." (No editor ever made him compress a story, or change a comma.) "Poverty and trouble in life; domestic infelicity," which is accurate. "Lack of sympathy in nature"—as kind a man as I ever met, yet he was out of touch with the broad range of human activities, as he himself states in Derleth's HPL, in an excerpt from a letter to me. "Austere character, spoiled by false pride." Surely he was austere in the finest meaning of the word, and just as surely was it false pride speaking when he wrote me how repugnant was the very idea of writing for money. "Self imposition and deception will mar the life." He did deceive himself into accepting limitations of his talent. The realism so apparent in his weird fiction would have made him distinguished in the fiction of every day life, which he professed himself to be unable to write, because of his "ignorance". "The native is distrustful of others, and lacking in self-confidence also, yet apt to assert his independence at inopportune moments." Many a MS was kept buried for years, because he lacked the confidence to send it out; one rejection depressed him disastrously; many a MS did finally sell and only because some friend urged, demanded that it be submitted. Yet he would stubbornly refuse to make minor changes or any concession at all. He would not even try to see whether facilitating things for an editor could be done without loss of artistic integrity.

"Much sickness, and a wasting of vital powers; a careful, watchful nature, seldom achieving any great work, but always laborious." Laborious indeed! For twenty-eight consecutive hours, HPL and I sat in my studio in New Orleans, the first time we'd ever met, while he criticized Tarbis of the Lake, minutely picking each phrase to pieces; charmingly, affably bringing up the most hair-splitting questions of verisimilitude, and the most remote also. Delightful, yet—laborious, and typical. Careful, too. Only once did I catch him in error: in The Call of Cthulhu, he had a police inspector in New Orleans living in a block of a street in the Vieux Carre where no residences existed, or could well exist. Warehouses and the L&N tracks interfered. We had a hearty chuckle on that one!

Already, we have left coincidence in the dust. But let's go further. Saturn is the lord of the first decan; and

Saturn is in the fifth degree of Virgo. William Lilly gives this description of one whose "significator", Saturn, is in that sign: "A person of tall, spare body, swarthy, dark or black hair, and it plentiful; a long head, solid countenance; generally unfortunate; inclined to melancholy, retaining anger; a projector of many curious matters to little purpose; studious, subtle, reserved."

As I recollect from a letter, he was five feet, eleven inches tall, though inclined to stoop, and so not looking his height; his hair was dark, though not notably plentiful; whoever has seen his picture as published by Arkham will agree with Lilly's description. I'd hardly call him swarthy, yet considering his sedentary life, he was inclined to be dark, and he had brown eyes.

Birth as early as 3:14 a. m. would exclude Leo as the ascendant; whereas had he been born later than 3:50 a. m., Uranus would have been in the Fourth rather than the Third House. The Uranian influence on the mental qualities would not have been as they actually were, since Third and Ninth notably affect mentality. Had he been born as late as 3:54 a. m., the second decan of Leo, ruled by Jupiter, would have been rising. Jupiter, in this nativity in Aquarius, indicates "middle stature, well set, corpulent, compact."

Now let us fill out the picture: "Sun in the First House: 'Honor and success. A proud disposition; frank, outspoken, generous; independent and firm. Love of display and publicity, accompanied by high motives.'"

"Saturn in the Second House: 'Business losses; thrifty nature; hard work for little gain; sometimes poverty.'"

"Mercury in the Third: 'Much activity; many short journeys; much writing; a busy mind, given to the pursuit of various knowledges, especially literature and science.'"

"Moon in the Third: 'Constant journeys; publicity of some sort; many changes of pursuit and occupation; curious and capricious fancies.'"

"Venus in Third: 'Strong inclination to the fine arts; success in letters and writings; peaceful relations among members of the family; amiable disposition, bright, fruitful intellect. Poetry, music, singing, and painting are among the pursuits of those under this influence.'" (HPL sketched admirably; did he ever paint?)

"Uranus in the Third: 'Wayward mind, curious and inventive; unpopular ideas which, if published, only incur severe loss and adverse criticism.'" (This last, if not taken too literally, describes the man's career until he was finally discovered; compared to the big success, in a material way, in the fiction world, his ideas were "unpopular"; and compared to what he might have written, they caused "severe loss" financially. Finally, in Derleth's HPL we learn how, in early boyhood, his unpopularity with his playmates drove him to books and study.)

"Mars in the Sixth: 'Inflammatory complaints in the bowels.' (Died of cancer of the intestine.) 'Extravagance in food and dress.'" (Not true—but he never had anything wherewith to be extravagant. However, his oft expressed wish that he lived in the Georgian period, so that he could dress in a way to accord with his tastes, betokened the desire for extravagance.)

"Jupiter in the Eighth: 'Marriage brings prosperity—the partner is or will be rich; gain by legacy; a happy death.'" (He did, I understand, have a small income from a granite quarry. I have had no first hand account of his closing days, or of the day of his death. Marriage brought him no prosperity.)

"Neptune in Eleventh: 'Seductive friends and alliances, unreliable advisors; treachery among supposed friends; losses and troubles thereby. The wife is liable to moral delinquency, sometimes making havoc among the native's friends. Strange and unaccountable attractions and associations.'" (No comment, other than that he was more often than not grossly underpaid for his collaboration-revision service. He considered it vulgar to dicker about splitting the proceeds of a collaboration; the mere thought of discussing the matter of dividing the check for Gates of the Silver Key made him squirm. I fancy it was a shock to him when I said, "Take seventy-five percent of the total—twenty-five percent will pay me for doing the typing and blocking out the initial sketch, and the six thousand word first draft.")

Uranus, in Libra, makes the native keen at reasoning, fond of travel, eccentric, ambitious; possessed of imagination, taste, intuition, and aesthetic faculties. Sometimes it leads to hasty marriage, with danger of estrangement or divorce. The native is prone to arouse criticisms, rivalry, opposition.

This is a skimpy sketch: it is not synthesized, nor is it keyed to the salient events of his life. My motive for making this investigation was, Lovecraft-like, to test, scientifically, astrology in general, and specifically, the method of "rectifying" horoscopes when the hour and minute of birth are not known. Inasmuch as HPL was one of the most striking characters I have ever known, I reasoned that his chart would contain unusual features permitting a ready "rectification" by working backward, from the personality to the stars, and so deducting the hour of his birth, and the minutes in a bracket not too wide. If through the circulation of *The Arkham Sampler* some HPL friend or relative (if any of these survive) be moved to investigate, and either confirm or contradict that he was born not much earlier or later than 3:50 a. m., I should be greatly obliged.

In closing, I submit this citation from Llewellyn George, the dean of American astrologers: "Your Sun sign in this incarnation will be your ascending sign in the next; that is, your present individuality or inherent qualities will then manifest outwardly as personality; it follows then that the present ascending sign was the Sun sign in the previous incarnation.

"When the Sun sign and the ascendant are the same, it indicates that the individual is repeating the experience (of the previous incarnation) and will continue to repeat until the lessons of life are heeded, and utilized as a step in the 'Jacob's ladder' to ascend toward higher realms of expression."

You will note that the sun was in Leo, 27th degree, and that the 9th degree of Leo was ascending at HPL's birth. From this I can only conclude that HPL in his next incarnation may again be born when the sun is in Leo, and Leo is ascending. For he was an inflexible and unchanging man; neither logic nor poverty could move or budge him, nor could pleas or persuasion. Not a stubborn man, and not an antagonistic man : anything but these— merely, a man who took a position and held that position. To the death and to the uttermost: amiably, pleasantly, cordially, but firmly.

Yet—when Harry Brobst and I bought beer and cooked a pot of East Indian curry at 66 College Street, July 5, 1933, HPL smiled and was friendly about our drinking. He had changed, over the years. There had been a time when the very mention of beer would have brought out all his sternness and disapproval. Seabury Quinn and HPL, so Quinn tells me, clashed on the matter of a cocktail served in defiance of prohibition. But the Lovecraft I knew was cordial in the presence of imbibers such as Brobst and I. He merely marveled, as a scientist, that any two men could share six bottles of beer and not fall on their faces. So, HPL may in his next incarnation be born under other signs. And I'd like to be born under such signs that I could see him oftener, and see more of him.

ABOUT THE AUTHOR

Edgar Hoffmann Trooper Price (July 3, 1898 – June 18, 1988) was an American writer of popular fiction (he was a self-titled 'fictioneer') for the pulp magazine marketplace. He collaborated with H. P. Lovecraft on "Through the Gates of the Silver Key."

Price was born at Fowler, California. Originally intending to be a career soldier, Price graduated from the United States Military Academy at West Point; he served in the American Expeditionary Force in World War I, and with the American military in Mexico and the Philippines. He was a champion fencer and boxer, an amateur Orientalist, and a student of the Arabic language; science-fiction author Jack Williamson, in his 1984 autobiography *Wonder's Child*, called E. Hoffmann Price a "real live soldier of fortune".

In his literary career, Hoffmann Price produced fiction for a wide range of publications, from *Argosy* to *Terror Tales*, from *Speed Detective* to *Spicy Mystery Stories*. Yet he was most readily identified as a *Weird Tales* writer, one of the group who wrote regularly for editor Farnsworth Wright, a group that included Lovecraft, Robert E. Howard, and Clark Ashton Smith. Price published 24 solo stories in *Weird Tales* between 1925 and 1950, plus three collaborations with Otis Adelbert Kline, and his work with Lovecraft, noted above.

His first sale was to *Droll Stories* in 1924, followed almost immediately by the first of scores of acceptances by *Weird Tales*, "The Rajah's Gift" (Jan 1925).

Some of Price's stories aroused controversy; "The Stranger from Kurdistan" (1925), a story which featured a dialogue between Christ and Satan, was criticized by some readers as blasphemous but proved popular with *Weird Tales* readers. (Lovecraft professed to find it especially powerful). "The Infidel's Daughter" (1927), a satire on the Ku Klux Klan, also angered some Southern readers, but Wright defended the story.

Price worked in a range of popular genres—including science fiction, horror, crime, and fantasy—but he was best known for adventure stories with Oriental settings and atmosphere. Price also contributed to Farnsworth Wright's short-lived magazine *The Magic Carpet* (1930–34), along with Kline, Howard, Smith, and other *Weird Tales* regulars.

Like many other pulp-fiction writers, Price could not support himself and his family on his income from literature. Living in New Orleans in the 1930s, he worked for a time for the Union Carbide Corporation. Nonetheless he managed to travel widely and maintain friendships with many other pulp writers, including Kline and Edmond Hamilton. On a trip to Texas in the mid-1930s, Price was the only pulp writer to meet Robert E. Howard face to face. He was also the only man known to have met Howard and also H.P. Lovecraft and Clark Ashton Smith (the great 'Triumvirate' of *Weird Tales* writers) in person. Over the course of his long life, Price made reminiscences of many significant figures in pulp fiction, Howard, Lovecraft, and Hamilton among them.

Late in life, Price experienced a major literary resurgence. In the 1970s and '80s he issued a series of SF, fantasy, and adventure novels, published in paperback; *The Devil Wives of Li Fong* (1979) is one noteworthy example. He also had published two collections of his pulp stories during his lifetime—*Strange Gateways* and *Far Lands, Other Days*.

Price was one of the first speakers at San Francisco's Maltese Falcon Society in 1981.

He received the World Fantasy Lifetime Achievement Award in 1984. A collection of his literary memoirs, *Book of the Dead: Friends of Yesteryear, Fictioneers & Others*, was published posthumously in 2001. His writing friends and colleagues included Richard L. Tierney, H.P. Lovecraft, August Derleth, Jack Williamson, Edmond Hamilton, Robert E. Howard, Clark Ashton Smith, Henry Kuttner, Seabury Quinn, Otis Adelbert Kline, Ralph Milne Farley, Robert Spencer Carr, and Farnsworth Wright among others.

Price died at Redwood City, California, in 1988.

www.ingramcontent.com/pod-product-compliance
Lightning Source LLC
Chambersburg PA
CBHW031309060426
42444CB00032B/912